Genie –
the Crash

Julie Sykes

Illustrated by Tony Blundell

OXFORD
UNIVERSITY PRESS

DUMFRIES & GALLOWAY LIBRARIES

AS238833

Askews & Holts	Feb-2014
JF	£6.30

1

Test time at the Three Wishes School

It was test time again at the Three Wishes School for genies.

Miss Genius put a pile of test papers in her cupboard. Then she beamed at the class.

'Tomorrow is your end of year test,' she said. 'Work hard and don't worry. Then you will all pass.'

Jem Stone groaned. He'd forgotten all about the test. Flying was sure to come up in the test and his magic carpet had a hole in it. He'd been meaning to fix it for ages. Now he'd have to spend all evening mending the hole. He wouldn't have time to practise for the test. But there was worse to come.

'Today we are going to practise flying our carpets,' said Miss Genius. 'Line up at the window with your carpets, class.'

Pearl stood up and accidentally-on-purpose trod on Jem's foot.

'Ouch!' he cried. 'Look out, clumsy clogs!'

'*Me?* Clumsy?' said Pearl, spitefully. '*You're* the most clumsy genie in the whole of the school, Jem Stone!'

Jem frowned. It was true. He didn't mean to be clumsy, but he did have a lot of accidents. Only last week, he'd fallen into the lake when the class were learning about frogs.

'Don't listen to Pearl,' said Pebble, kindly.

Pebble was Jem's best friend and she didn't like Pearl at all.

Miss Genius frowned at Jem and Pebble. 'No talking!'

Miss Genius went on, 'Pearl. Thank you for tidying up my room after class, yesterday. You can go first.'

Pearl smirked. 'Out of my way,' she said.

'Teacher's pet,' hissed Jem.

'*Don't* listen to her,' said Pebble. 'She's not worth it.'

Pearl had the best magic carpet in the school but she wasn't very good at flying. She almost bumped into the window when she flew out of the classroom. Her carpet wobbled and then she was gone.

'I can catch her, easy peasy,' said Jem. He jumped onto his carpet, and shouted, 'Fly!'

'Mind that hole!' Pebble told him.

'I will,' said Jem, and he whizzed out of the window.

2

Jem gets into trouble

Jem's old carpet could not fly as fast as Pearl's posh new one, and the hole made it even slower. But Jem was much better at flying than Pearl and soon he was just behind her.

He was getting ready to overtake, when Pearl flew her carpet in front of him.

'Oi!' shouted Jem. 'Look out! I'm trying to get past.'

But Pearl wouldn't move out of the way. When Jem flew left, she flew left, too. When Jem flew right, Pearl flew right. When Jem flew up, Pearl flew up.

Then Jem had a clever idea. He would fly *under* Pearl's carpet! It would be dangerous but Jem hoped he could do it.

'Carpet, fly down,' he said.

Pearl heard him and grinning spitefully, she flew her carpet down, too.

Jem tried to fly down even faster, so Pearl wouldn't hit him. But his foot got stuck in the hole. He tried and tried to tug it free and the carpet wobbled closer and closer to Pearl.

BANG! The two carpets crashed.
Then Jem and his carpet began to fall.

Jem could see Miss Genius standing
on the playground. He tried to move
the carpet out of her way but the hole
was making it very hard to steer.

Miss Genius was a bit deaf and she
hadn't noticed Jem was about to fall on
her head.

Jem did some fast thinking. Spells were against the school rules. He would be in big trouble if Miss Stick, the head teacher, found out. But he had to do something, or he would crash onto Miss Genius.

'*Carpet*,' Jem wished,
'*Please land beside her,
As softly as a spider.*'

There was another bang and a cloud of green smoke. Jem landed with a bump.

Something small ran over his hand and then scuttled away.

Pebble helped him up and she looked very upset.

'What did you do that for?' she cried. 'Why did you turn Miss Genius into a spider?'

'I didn't,' said Jem, hotly.

'You did!'

'Didn't!'

'Did!'

'Didn't, didn't, didn't! I wished for my carpet to land *beside* her,' said Jem.

'Well it sounded as if you wished our teacher into a *spider*, and now she *is* one,' said Pebble. 'Poor Miss Genius. Turn her back again, quickly!'

'I'm trying to!' cried Jem.

He knew he had to act very fast.
Miss Genius mustn't find out that he
had used a spell on her. If she found
out that Jem had turned her into a
spider she would be very cross. She
might not let him take the test
tomorrow. That would be awful. Jem
would have to stay in the beginners'
class for another year.

But as Jem began the spell, the school cat came running towards them. His green eyes were lit up like lamps.

'It's Claws!' cried Pebble. 'Quick! Jem, he's after the spider. He mustn't catch Miss Genius!'

Jem tried to grab the cat, but he slipped through Jem's fingers.

3

Where is Miss Genius?

Jem and Pebble raced after the cat as
he headed across the playground after
the spider.

The cat was quick but the spider was
quicker. It scuttled across the
playground and into the school. Then
it slipped under the door of the girls'
room. The cat spat, crossly, and put his
paw under the door.

'Oh, no, you don't!' cried Jem. He picked the cat up and took him back to the playground. Then he shut the school door so that the cat couldn't get back inside and ran back to the girls' room. Pebble was waiting for him.

'She's under there,' said Pebble, pointing to a small cupboard. 'Look, you can just see one of her legs.'

Jem picked up a glass and handed it to Pebble.

'I'm going to move the cupboard. Put this glass over the spider to stop her running away again. It won't hurt her.'

All of a sudden, the door burst open.

Pearl came in followed by the rest of the class. 'Get away from my things, Jem Stone,' she yelled.

'Don't be silly, Pearl,' said Pebble. 'Jem is only trying to catch Miss Genius.'

'It's *my* cupboard. *I'll* catch her,' said Pearl, angrily. 'Come away from my things or I'll tell Miss Stick, the head teacher, what you did to Miss Genius. She'll throw you out of school, Jem Stone. You know it's against the rules to do spells on the teachers!'

'Oh, go away!' said Pebble.

She pushed Pearl out of the room and locked the door.

'You can't lock me out of the girls' room!' yelled Pearl and she rattled the door handle. 'I'm going to get Miss Stick. Then you'll be sorry.'

Pebble looked worried. 'Hurry up, Jem. We haven't got much time.'

Jem pushed the cupboard very
carefully. A piece of paper
fluttered out from
under it.

'Can you see the spider?' he asked.

'No,' said Pebble.
Jem pushed the cupboard again.

'*There* she is!' yelled Pebble, excitedly. 'Move it again, Jem.'

Jem moved the cupboard again.

Pebble lifted up the glass and put it carefully over the spider. 'Got her!' cried Pebble.

Everybody in the room cheered.

Jem raced over to Pebble. He was in such a hurry to turn the spider back into Miss Genius that he tripped and crashed into Pebble.

'Look out!' Pebble cried. She was still holding the glass against the floor.

'Sorry!' said Jem, and he started to make a new spell.

'*Spider, goodbye, Miss Genius, hi.*'

There was a loud POP and a cloud of green smoke. When it cleared, Miss Genius was back to herself. Well, almost. She was sitting on the floor with a glass on her head.

4

Miss Genius has a surprise

All of a sudden, there was a bang on the door. It sounded angry.

'Let me in,' shouted the head teacher.

Jem opened the door. He knew he was in very big trouble now. Miss Stick sounded very cross. Pearl was with her, looking smug.

'There he is!' she said. 'In the girls' room, and poor Miss Genius …'

Pearl stopped and stared at her teacher in surprise. Miss Genius was holding up a piece of paper.

'What was *this* doing under your cupboard, Pearl?' she asked.

'I ... I ...' For once, Pearl was lost for words.

'This is a copy of tomorrow's test paper,' went on Miss Genius. 'When did you take it? Was it when you tidied up my room after school, yesterday? And I thought you were being helpful!'

Miss Stick took the test paper from Miss Genius. She looked very cross. 'Does this mean you were going to cheat, Pearl Gates?' she said. 'Come to my office!'

She turned to Miss Genius and said, 'Pearl cannot take the end of year test, now. She will have to stay in the beginners' class.'

Miss Stick marched from the room with Pearl following her.

Nobody said anything for a moment and then Miss Genius smiled. 'Class is over. You can use the rest of the day to practise for the test.'

'Yes!' shouted everybody. 'Thanks, Miss Genius.'

'You can thank me by getting top marks, tomorrow,' said Miss Genius. 'And Jem, you must be *very* careful with your spells. You know, I might *accidentally* turn you into a fly.'

Everybody laughed and Jem laughed too. He was glad he wasn't in trouble for turning Miss Genius into a spider.

'Come on,' said Pebble, taking Jem's arm. 'Let's go and practise for our test.'

'Later,' said Jem, heading for the door. 'But first of all, I've got a hole in my carpet that needs fixing.'

About the author

I live in Hampshire with my
husband, our three children
and a very big dog. I don't
have much spare time, but
when I do, I like reading,
walking and cooking.

The idea for Jem Stone
Genie came when I was
thinking about the best way to travel to school.
Riding on a flying carpet seemed an exciting
way to get there. Children would then have to
take a flying test instead of a cycling one!